Observe, admire, remember ...
Save the beauty for my children!

Photography, design
Bogdan KLADNIK

Text
Marjeta KERŠIČ - SVETEL

English version
Henrik CIGLIČ

German version
Wolfgang ZITTA

Italian version
SKRIVANEK d.o.o.

Published by
ZAKLAD, Ljubljana

Representative
Bogdan KLADNIK

For more information on our books write to:
Založba ZAKLAD, Čižmanova 6, 1211 Ljubljana, Slovenija
or call: +386 (0) 41 633 328
or visit: www.zaklad.si

Lithography
Camera, Ljubljana

Print and binding
Tisk Žnidarič, Kranj

CIP - Kataložni zapis o publikaciji
Narodna in univerzitetna knjižnica, Ljubljana

908(497.4)(084.12)
77.047.1(497.4)

KLADNIK, Bogdan
Slovenija / [photography] Bogdan Kladnik ; [text] Marjeta Keršič - Svetel ; [translation Henrik Ciglič, German version Wolfgang Zitta, Italian version Skrivanek]. - Ljubljana : Zaklad, 2006

ISBN 961-6266-19-5

220930304

Front cover: A view at the Koritnica Valley
Pages 6/7: Haymaking in the Loška Valley

Slovenia

Not long ago, I found myself in a motley company sitting at a conference, at which experts from all over the world took part. Soon, they began to explain where they come from: Canada, Switzerland, United States, China ... »Slovenia? Where on earth is this?« somebody asked inquisitively when it was my turn to tell them something about my origin. »I know!« triumphantly declared my new acquaintance from the States. »I've been there already! It's on the way from Venice to Vienna! A small country ... no more than a couple of hours drive. Unfortunately, I only drove through it – but it seemed a very attractive country to me. With a multitude of forests!«

»And it truly is beautiful! In terms of its forest density, we are ranked the third in Europe – immediately after Finland and Sweden. Furthermore, our forests happen to be very diverse, from beech-fir to floodplain oak forests, from Austrian pine woodlands to montane larch groves ... and owing to their sustainable management they are very attractive indeed! We can even boast some virgin forests, still inhabited by large carnivores, such as bears, lynxes and even few wolves ...« I began to explain to my new companions about my native land. About Slovenia, which is indeed small but uniquely picturesque and diverse. I kept telling them about the mountains of steep rockwalls and secluded trails, about the realm of Triglav and its legendary Goldenhorn, about the highest Slovene mountain, which is such an important symbol to us, the Slovenes, that we have placed it in the national coat-of-arms ... about the mountain valleys where you can scent the gorgeously fragrant hay during the summer ... and about the autumn tranquillity in the Trenta Valley sinking in the shadows of the surrounding mountains. I told them much about the variegated meadows, where you can listen to larks and crickets during the summer, about the friendly hillocks with orchards and vineyards, where the kind locals will gladly invite you to their vineyard cottages to taste their premium wines they are righteously proud of. About the streams and rivers either roaring in the deep gorges or lazily meandering in the lowlands, about the torrents and watercourses where alder trees are reflected in their quite branches, where frogs are croaking and dragonflies flying tirelessly, and where you can even see, with a bit of luck, a playful otter ... I acquainted them with the silence of underground caves, with the mysterious world of karst waters, intermittent lakes and unusual animals inured to the eternal darkness ... how the sea roars under the steep walls of our no more than a good forty kilometres long coast, and how salt is still being harvested there under the scorching sun, just as centuries ago. I told them about the scent of the sea, olive oil, cornfields, flocks of sheep, soil ... and honey. And about the huge and slightly melancholy fool moon rising in the summer months above the lowland along the Mura river.

»You really must love your Slovenia, considering you're telling us about it with such incredible enthusiasm!«
I felt slightly embarrassed when my new acquaintance interrupted my monologue.
I admit: whenever I begin to speak about my homeland and its countless beautiful nooks, I get carried away.

This piece of land, squeezed between the Alps and the Mediterranean, between the Pannonian Plain and the Dinarides, is something special indeed. Not only due to its exceptionally diverse and well preserved nature, but also owing to its varied past and cultural heritage. It seems that it is not just a pure coincidence that it was this very country in which one of the oldest instruments in the entire world has been discovered by archaeologists – the bone flute, attributed even to a Neanderthal musician. Culture and creativity – this is what has kept us, the Slovenes, who acquired our modern independent state only as late as in 1991, as an authentic nation through the long history of foreign rule. To the great pleasure of poets and those in love, we have persisted in our language and its very special feature – dual form. »Jaz (I) – midva (two of us) – mi (we)!« A linguistic peculiarity that says much about our character! As diverse as Slovene nature are also Slovenia's dialects, its cuisine, architecture, customs ... and the modern cultural creativity drawing its inspiration from all of these mosaic-like riches of diversity.

Today, the world is just a single, global village. African lions, the Grand Canyon in Colorado, whales, the Himalayas, and the latest modern art exhibition in Paris – everything comes so cosily to our living rooms, to the TV screen or computer monitor. This is why at times we forget, due to the multitude of world attractions and creative achievements supplied by the media, that the genuine everyday life is in fact full of highly interesting things – all you have to do is to set out on a short journey and discover them. And Slovenia is as made for this very purpose! Everything is so nicely at hand ... In the morning, you can ski down the upland snows, in the afternoon you can dip your feet in the sea – and if this is still not enough, you can finally crawl into some picturesque underground cave full of calcite jewellery and eternal darkness, where it does not matter when the sun goes down on the surface outside.

It is even nicer, however, if you take time and simply surrender yourself to nothing but just strolling around. Through murmuring forests, along old cart tracks, past old homesteads, where one can scent tiny, old variety apples and must pears in the autumn months ... past little churches that stand virtually on every hillock, each of them representing a little jewel of art of the past centuries ... along narrow little streets of mediaeval towns, past old castles with stories about lust for power and fights between noble families ... or about disappointment in love, the lord of the castle's daughter turned into a snake, and a dreadful dragon conquered by a courageous shepherd ...

Slovenia is a multitude of things: it is a view from the top of Mt Triglav with a never-ending sequel of rocky summits, fishermen rejoicing at daybreak while gazing at their nets full of mullets, frolicsome girls waiting for their dates at the foot of the monument to poet France Prešeren in the very centre of Ljubljana, and spirited Lipizzan horses in karst meadows ... Slovenia is wakening up with the singing of birds, it is an eternal silence of the snowbound forest, murmuring of mountain streams, fields of sunflowers and storks nesting on the top of old chimneys ... and placid wisdom on the face of a horny-handed granny, talking to the sun on a bench in front of her homestead.

Still, Slovenia is much, much more than that – which means that we all have to discover it by ourselves, to get acquainted with it and grow fond of it. Then, it will be like bread. You never get tired of it, and if you are far from it you miss it so much that it hurts.

Velika Korita on the Soča river

Slowenien

Es ist noch nicht lange her, dass ich in einer bunten Gesellschaft von Teilnehmern einer Konferenz saß, an der Fachleute aus aller Herren Länder teilgenommen hatten. Jeder erzählte, woher er kommt: aus Kanada, der Schweiz, den USA, aus China ... „Slowenien? Wo liegt denn das?“ fragte jemand neugierig, als ich sagte, woher ich komme. „Ich weiß es!“ erklärte rasch mein neuer Bekannter aus den USA mit triumphierender Miene. „Ich war schon dort! Es liegt auf dem Weg von Venedig nach Wien! Ein kleines Land ... kaum ein paar Autostunden. Leider bin ich nur vorbeigefahren – aber es sieht sehr schön aus. Viel Wald!“

„Es ist wirklich schön, unser Slowenien! Nach dem Anteil der Wälder liegt es an dritter Stelle in Europa – gleich nach Finnland und Schweden. Unsere Wälder sind sehr vielfältig – von Buchen- und Tannenwäldern bis zu Eichenwäldern in Auenlandschaften, von Schwarzkiefer- bis zu alpinen Lärchenwäldern ... und wegen der naturnahen Bewirtschaftung sind die slowenischen Wälder tatsächlich schön! Wir haben sogar einige Urwaldgebiete ... und in unseren Wäldern leben noch große Raubtiere – Bären und Luchse und sogar ein paar Wölfe ...“, begann ich meinen neuen Bekannten von dem Land zu erzählen, in dem ich zu Hause bin. Von Slowenien, das wirklich klein ist, aber malerisch und vielfältig wie nur wenige Länder auf der Welt. Ich erzählte ihnen von Bergen mit Steilwänden und einsamen Pfaden, vom Triglaver Reich des sagenumwobenen Goldhorns und von Sloweniens höchstem Berg, der für die Slowenen ein so wichtiges Symbol darstellt, dass er das Staatswappen schmückt ... und von Gebirgstälern, wo es im Sommer nach gemähtem Heu duftet ... und von der herbstlichen Stille des Trentatals, das in den Schatten der umliegenden Berge taucht. Ich erzählte ihnen von bunten Wiesen, wo man sommers den Lerchen und Grillen zuhören kann, von lieblichen Hügeln mit Obst- und Weingärten, wo man von freundlichen Einheimischen gern in ihr Weinberghäuschen eingeladen wird, die guten Weine zu kosten, auf die sie mit Recht stolz sind. Und von Bächen und Flüssen, die in tiefen Schluchten tosen, und von trägen und verträumten, von reißenden und solchen, in denen sich in ruhigen Armen Erlen spiegeln, wo Frösche quaken, Libellen umherschwirren und wo man mit viel Glück sogar auf eine verspielte Otter treffen kann ... Ich erzählte ihnen von der Stille unterirdischer Höhlen, von der geheimnisvollen Welt der Karstgewässer und periodischen Seen und von ungewöhnlichen, an ewiges Dunkel gewöhnten Tieren ... und davon, wie die Wellen unter den Steilwänden unserer kaum mehr als 40 km langen Meeresküste ans Ufer schlagen und wie in der Sonnenhitze dort noch immer wie vor Jahrhunderten Salz gewonnen wird. Vom Duft nach Meer und Olivenöl, nach Kornfeldern und Schafherden ... nach Erde und Honig. Und vom riesigen, ein bisschen melancholischen Vollmond, der in den Sommernächten über der Ebene an der Mur aufsteigt.

„Sie müssen aber wirklich Ihr Land lieben, wenn Sie von all dem so begeistert erzählen!“

Es war mir ein wenig unangenehm, als mein neuer Bekannter meine Erzählflut unterbrach.

Ich gestehe, wenn ich von meinem Heimatland und seinen unzähligen schönen Gegenden zu erzählen beginne, gerate ich leicht ins Schwärmen.

Moon bay and the cliffs of Strunjan

A
GIUSEPPE TARTINI
L'ISTRIA
MDCCCLXXXXVI

Dieses Fleckchen Erde zwischen Alpen und Mittelmeerraum, zwischen Ungarischem Tiefland und Dinarischem Gebirge ist tatsächlich etwas Besonderes. Nicht nur wegen seiner ungemein vielfältigen und gut erhaltenen Natur, sondern auch wegen seiner bewegten Geschichte und seines Kulturerbes. Es scheint mir kein reiner Zufall zu sein, dass die Archäologen gerade in Slowenien eines der ältesten Musikinstrumente der Welt gefunden haben - eine beinerne Flöte, die sogar einem musikalischen Neandertaler zugeschrieben wird. Kultur und Kreativität - das ist es, was uns Slowenen, die wir unseren unabhängigen Staat erst 1991 erhalten haben, durch die lange Geschichte der Fremdherrschaft als eigenständiges Volk erhalten hat. Zur großen Freude der Dichtern und Verliebten haben wir durchgehalten mit unserer Sprache und seiner Besonderheit, dem Dual: „Ich - wir zwei- wir!" Eine sprachliche Besonderheit, die manches über unseren Charakter sagt! So vielfältig wie seine Natur sind auch Sloweniens Mundarten, Esskultur, Baukunst, Brauchtum ... und sein heutiges Kulturschaffen, das aus all diesem mosaikartigen Reichtum schöpft.

Die Welt ist heutzutage ein einziges großes, globales Dorf. Afrikanische Löwen, der Grand Canyon in Colorado, Wale, der Himalaja und die neueste Ausstellung zeitgenössischer Kunst in Paris - alles gelangt schön in unser Wohnzimmer, auf den Bildschirm des Fernsehers oder Computers. Bei der Fülle von Weltsensationen und kreativen Überschüssen, mit denen uns die Medien überhäufen, vergessen wir deshalb zuweilen, dass das echte, tägliche Leben voller Reize und Schönheiten ist - man muss sich nur auf den Weg machen und sie entdecken. Slowenien ist wie geschaffen dafür! Alles ist hier so schön versammelt und in Reichweite ... Am Morgen kann man im Hochgebirge Ski laufen, am Nachmittag die Füße ins Meer strecken - und wenn es noch nicht genug des Schönen ist, kann man schließlich noch in eine malerische, mit Tropfstein geschmückte unterirdische Höhle steigen, wo so oder so ewiges Dunkel herrscht und es ganz egal ist, wann oben die Sonne untergeht.

Noch schöner ist es aber, wenn man sich Zeit nimmt und sich einfach dem Wandern hingibt. Durch rauschende Wälder, auf alten Fahrwegen, vorbei an Bauernhöfen inmitten von Obstgärten, wo es im Herbst nach kleinen Äpfeln alter Sorten und Birnen duftet ... Vorbei an kleinen Kirchen, die fast auf jedem kleinen Hügel stehen und von denen jede ein Kleinod vergangener Zeiten darstellt ... Durch enge Gassen mittelalterlicher Städte, vorbei an alten Burgen mit Geschichten von Machtgier und Rivalitäten zwischen Adelsfamilien ...oder von einer unglücklichen Liebe, von der in eine Schlange verzauberten Tochter eines Schlossherrn und von einem schrecklichen Drachen, den ein mutiger Hirte besiegt hat ...

Slowenien - das ist der Ausblick vom Gipfel des Triglav - endlose Reihen imposanter Kalkfelsen und glazialer Täler. Slowenien - das sind die Fischer, die sich am frühen Morgen über die vollen Netze mit Meeräschen freuen, die ausgelassenen Mädchen, die auf eine Verabredung unter dem Prešeren-Denkmal im Zentrum von Ljubljana warten, und die ungestümen weißen Pferde auf den Karstwiesen ... Slowenien - das ist das Aufwachen bei Vogelgezwitscher, die unendliche Stille eines verschneiten Waldes, wenn es in dicken Flocken schneit, das Plätschern der Gebirgsbäche, die Sonnenblumenfelder und die Störche, die auf alten Schornsteinen nisten ... und die weise Gelassenheit auf dem Gesicht einer Großmutter mit schwieligen Händen, die auf einer Bank vor dem Bauernhaus mit der Sonne ein Zwiegespräch hält.

Und noch vieles, vieles mehr ist Slowenien - jeder muss es selbst entdecken, kennen und lieben lernen. Dann ist es wie Brot. Man wird seiner nie überdrüssig, und wenn man weit weg ist, vermisst man es so, dass es wehtut.

Piran, the statue of Giuseppe Tartini

Slovenia

Qualche tempo fa mi trovavo seduta nel gruppo eterogeneo dei partecipanti ad una riunione cui avevano preso parte degli esperti provenienti da ogni angolo del mondo. Ognuno stava spiegando da dove veniva. Chi dal Canada, chi dalla Svizzera, dagli Stati Uniti, dalla Cina ... "Slovenia? Ma dov'è?" chiese qualcuno, evidentemente incuriosito, quando dissi da che Paese venivo. "Io lo so!" rispose con un tono quasi trionfante un mio nuovo conoscente degli Stati Uniti d'America. "Ci sono stato una volta! Si trova sulla strada tra Venezia e Vienna! Uno staterello piccolo ... lo si attraversa in poche ore di macchina. Purtroppo ci sono solo passato - ma a vederlo così sembra un bel Paese. Pieno di boschi!"

"La nostra Slovenia è veramente bella! Siamo al terzo posto in Europa per percentuale di boschi - subito dopo la Finlandia e la Svezia. Le nostre foreste sono molto varie - dai boschi di faggi e abeti a boschi di querce, dai boschi di pino negro ai boschetti di larice in montagna ... e grazie ad una gestione ecologica i boschi sloveni sono veramente stupendi. Si sono conservate addirittura delle zone di foresta vergine ... e nei nostri boschi vivono anche grandi animali selvatici - orsi, linci e addirittura lupi ..." iniziai così a presentare ai miei nuovi conoscenti la mia patria. La Slovenia, che è sì piccola, ma pittoresca e variegata, come pochi altri Paesi al mondo. Raccontai delle montagne con le loro pareti scoscese e sentieri solitari, del regno del Tricorno del leggendario "Zlatorog", il camoscio dalle corna d'oro, un simbolo talmente importante per gli sloveni da essere raffigurato nello stemma nazionale ... e delle valli di montagna, che d'estate odorano di fieno tagliato ... oppure della tranquillità che regna nella Val Trenta, immersa nell'ombra delle vette circostanti. Raccontai loro dei prati variopinti, dove d'estate di possono sentire le allodole e i grilli, delle graziose colline ricoperte di frutteti e vigneti dove i contadini invitano volentieri il passante nella loro capanna ad assaggiare ottimi vini, dei quali vanno particolarmente fieri.

Raccontai dei ruscelli e dei fiumi, gorgoglianti negli anfratti e pigramente sognanti, di quelli vivaci e tumultuosi e di quelli nelle cui acque tranquille si specchiano gli ontani, dove gracidano le rane, dove si librano nell'aria le libellule e dove, con molta fortuna, ci si può imbattere in qualche lontra giocherellona ... Raccontai loro del silenzio delle grotte, del mondo misterioso delle acque carsiche, dei laghi intermittenti e degli strani animali abituati all'oscurità eterna ... e di come mugghiano le onde che vanno ad infrangersi sulle pareti rocciose dei nostri 40 km di costa, di come, nella calura estiva, si raccolga il sale marino secondo i procedimenti antichi di secoli. Descrissi il profumo del mare e dell'olio d'oliva, dei campi di grano e delle greggi di pecore ... di terra e di miele. E dell'enorme e un po' malinconica luna piena che, nelle notti estive, splende sulla pianura del Mura.

"Certo che deve proprio amarla tanto questa sua Slovenia, dal modo entusiasta con cui ne parla!"
Mi sembrò, a dire il vero, un po' inopportuno il modo in cui il mio nuovo conoscente aveva interrotto il mio racconto.
Lo ammetto: quando comincio a parlare della mia terra natia e delle sue innumerevoli bellezze, mi lascio prendere la mano.

Pages 12/13: Piran during sunset
Left: Bohinj, Church of St. John

Questo pezzetto di mondo, incastonato tra le Alpi e il Mediterraneo, tra la pianura Pannonica e i monti Dinarici, è veramente qualcosa di speciale. Non soltanto per la sua natura estremamente varia e ben conservata, ma anche per il suo movimentato passato e per il suo ricco patrimonio culturale. Ritengo che non sia un caso se gli archeologi hanno ritrovato proprio in Slovenia uno degli strumenti musicali più antichi al mondo - uno zufolo d'osso, attribuito addirittura all'uomo di Neanderthal. Cultura e creatività - questo è ciò che ha permesso a noi sloveni, che abbiamo ottenuto l'indipendenza del nostro Stato soltanto nel 1991, di mantenere la nostra identità di popolo nonostante le varie dominazioni straniere che si sono susseguite nel corso della storia. Per la gioia dei poeti e delle coppie di innamorati abbiamo conservato, nella nostra lingua, la particolarità del duale. "Jaz (io) - midva (noi due) - mi (noi)". Una particolarità linguistica che la dice lunga sul nostro carattere. Tanto variegata è la natura in Slovenia, quanto lo è la situazione dei dialetti, della cultura gastronomica, dell'architettura, degli usi e costumi, nonché della creatività dei tempi moderni che attinge a questo mosaico culturale, in tutte le sue sfaccettature.

Il mondo è, al giorno d'oggi, un unico, grande villaggio globale. I leoni africani, il Grand Canyon in Colorado, le balene, l'Himalaja e l'ultima mostra di arte contemporanea a Parigi - tutto ciò confluisce quotidianamente nel salotto di casa nostra, sullo schermo di un televisore o di un computer. Perciò, distratti dalla sovrabbondanza di attrazioni e stimoli creativi che giungono da tutto il mondo con cui ci bombardano i media, dimentichiamo talvolta che la vita vera e quotidiana è altrettanto piena di cose interessanti e belle - basta solo mettersi in viaggio e scoprirle. La Slovenia è il luogo ideale per questo. Tutto è così bello, tutto vicino e a portata di mano ... Al mattino si può sciare sulla neve d'alta montagna e al pomeriggio si possono immergere i piedi nell'acqua di mare - e se non basta, si può scendere e strisciare tra le splendide stalattiti e stalagmiti di qualche grotta, dove l'oscurità regna sovrana, indipendentemente se in superficie splende o no il sole.

Ma, meglio di tutto, se ci si dedica esclusivamente a gironzolare, guardandosi intorno. Nei boschi fruscianti, su vecchie strade sterrate, passando davanti alle fattorie in mezzo ai frutteti, dove in autunno profuma di piccole mele delle vecchie varietà e di pere da sidro ... Passando accanto alle chiesette che si trovano in cima a quasi ogni collinetta e che sono vere e proprie perle di arte delle epoche passate ... Per gli stretti vicoli dei centri storici delle città medievali, accanto a vecchi castelli con le loro storie di potere, di lotte e scontri tra le famiglie della nobiltà ... o storie di amori infelici, di fanciulle incantate dal serpente e dal terribile drago, sconfitto dal coraggioso pastore ...

Slovenia è anche la vista che si apre dalla cima del monte Tricorno - un'infinita distesa di vette di roccia calcarea e di valli glaciali. Slovenia sono anche i pescatori che, di mattina presto, raccolgono felici le reti piene di cefali; sono le ragazze allegre che aspettano qualcuno sotto il monumento di Prešeren nel centro di Lubiana, sono gli irruenti cavalli bianchi sui prati del Carso ... Slovenia è svegliarsi col canto degli uccelli, è l'infinito silenzio del bosco innevato quando cadono i fiocchi di neve, è il gorgoglio dei ruscelli di montagna, sono i campi di girasoli e le cicogne che fanno il loro nido sui vecchi comignoli... è la tranquilla saggezza sul volto di una vecchia donna dalle mani callose che, seduta sulla panca davanti casa, sta a parlare con il sole.

Ma la Slovenia non è solo questo, è qualcos'altro - che ognuno di noi deve scoprire, conoscere e apprezzare di persona. La Slovenia è come il pane. Non ti annoia mai e, quando ne sei lontano, ti manca fino a stare male.

Cowherd's Ball at Bohinj

Above: The Upper Sava Valley with the Kranjska gora ski resort
Pages 18/19: View of Lake Bled from Osojnica

A homestead "Pri Maselcu" in the Soča Valley

The Veliki Kozjak Waterfall near Kobarid

Divje jezero (Wild Lake) is our deepest karst spring, similar to Vaucluse in France

Ljubljana - the Capital of Slovenia
with about 300,000 inhabitants

Kranj - the biggest town in the Upper Carniola

Maribor is the second largest Slovene city

Ptuj on the Drava river is the oldest town in Slovenia

The 118 km long Kolpa is a dividing line between Slovenia and Croatia
Right: Peričnik Waterfall in the Vrata Valley

On the top of Mt Viševnik (2,050 m)

Siberian husky Tas under the top of Mt Vajnež (2,104 m)

A homestead in the Trenta Valley
Left: Double hayracks, called "toplars", at Studor

The magnificent Škocjan Caves in the vicinity of Divača are amongst the most prominent caves in the world. In 1986, they were inscribed on Unesco's world heritage list

Schmidl Hall, where a visitor to the Škocjan Caves sees the daylight again

Loška Valley near Lake Cerknica
Left: The famous intermittent Lake Cerknica

The Karst is the land of rock as well as the land of Teran wine

Karst landscape near Križ

The Možnica gorge

The Mlinarica gorge

A homestead in the Idrijca Valley
Left: The Idrijca river

On the Velika Planina

The high summer pastures on Velika Planina

Srednja vas at Bohinj

Sv. Andrej near Sežana
Left: Ptujska gora - the famous gothic Church of the Virgin Mary

The source of the Kropa in the Voje Valley

The Šteberk source at Lake Cerknica

The Dominek home in Gorišnica near Ptuj

Jeruzalem winegrowing hills

The Soča river near Srpenica

Above: View of Vipavski križ from the air
Pages 56/57: Slovenia is the land of marvellous Lipica horses

The Batič vineyards near Šempas in the Vipava Valley

Spring in the Vipava Valley

Above: Sv. Ožbalt near Luče
Right: A unique way of hay drying at Loški potok

View from Mt Triglav (2,864 m)
Left: The ridge leading to the top of Mt Triglav

The Postojna Caves are no doubt the most prominent among all Slovene caves

Magnificient Predjama Castle, 10km northwest of Postojna, was built into the mouth of an enormous 14km long cave.

Sunset above Ljubljana

Sv. Janez near Logatec

The Savinja Waterfall -
a magnificient
90m high waterfall
in the Logarska Valley

Among the competent judges of montane countryside, the Logarska Valley is renowned as an extremely attractive mountain valley

Above: Kostanjevica - A former Cistercian monastery with the "Forma Viva" art colony
Left: Novo mesto - the biggest town in the Lower Carniola with about 20,000 inhabitants, situated along one of the meanders of the Krka river

The Pleterje Carthusian monastery

Vineyards, rising above the Pleterje monastery
Pages 74/75: The slopes of Sleme below Slemenova Špica

Slovenija at a glance

Territory area: 20.273 sq. km
Population: 2 million
Population density: 98 inhabitants/sq. km
Capital: Ljubljana, population 300.000
Constitutional order: parliamentary republic
Official language: Slovene - as well as Italian and Hungarian in areas with mixed population
Currency: EUR
Religion: predominantly Roman Catholic
Climate: Alpine, Continental, Mediterranean
Border length: 1.207 km
Coast length: 47 km
The highest point: Mt. Triglav (2.864 m)
The longest river: Sava (221 km - from its source to the national border)
Waterfalls: over 300 with permanent water flow
The highest waterfall: Čedca (130 m)
Lakes: over 200
The largest lake: Cerknica (32 sq. km) - karst intermittent
Karst caves: over 8.600 registrated
The longest cave: Postojnska (19,5 km)
The deepest pothole: Čehi (-1.533 m)
Vrtiglavica (-642 m) - the deepest entrance pothole on Earth
Zlatorog (-365 m) - the deepest inner pothole on Earth

Accessibility:

By air: Ljubljana Airport - Brnik, 23 km from the city, www.lju-airport.si
Several direct flights a day to/from major European hubs and other destinations.
Most of the flights are operated by the national airline Adria Airways, www.adria-airways.com
By train: daily services to larger cities in neighbouring countries, www.slo-zeleznice.si
By car: good motorway and main road links to the major border crossings.
Road distances to Ljubljana: Venice 220 km • Milan 470 km • Zagreb 135 km • Budapest 440 km • Salzburg 280 km • Vienna 370 km • München 400 km • Zurich 630 km • Belgrade 540 km • Prague 610 km

Left: Autumn colours in the Krma Valley

Marjeta Keršič - Svetel

Cultural and artistic creativity is part of her family's tradition (her grandfather was a composer, mother an actress, father a sculptor), the same as her great love for nature and mountains (both parents were mountaineers).
After graduating in history and ethnology from Ljubljana University, she worked for almost 20 years for TV Slovenia as an author and editor of documentary broadcasts. For her authorial work in the series entitled »Mountains and People«, she received several awards at home and at film festivals abroad. Out of great wish to advance, with her expert knowledge, her affection for nature and particularly wilderness (may this be mountains, sea, forests or caves), she opted for post-graduate studies at the Biotechnical Faculty in Ljubljana and Birkbeck College of London University. After leaving TV Slovenia, she has worked as freelance journalist and lecturer.

Kulturelles und künstlerisches Schaffen gehört zu ihrer Familientradition (Großvater Komponist, Mutter Schauspielerin, Vater Bildhauer), genauso wie die große Liebe zur Natur und zu den Bergen (die Eltern waren auch passionierte Alpinisten). Nach dem Studium der Geschichte und Ethnologie war sie fast 20 Jahre lang als Dokumentaristin und Redakteurin bei der Slowenischen Fernsehanstalt tätig. Für ihre Dokumentarsendungen der Reihe Gore in ljudje (Berge und Menschen) erhielt sie den Viktor-Preis für hervorragende mediale Leistungen und zahlreiche Auszeichnungen auf ausländischen Filmfestivals. Vom Wunsch geleitet, ihre Naturverbundenheit und vor allem ihre Liebe zur Wildnis (seien es Berge, Meer, Wälder oder Höhlen) durch Fachkenntnisse zu vertiefen, hat sie sich zum Postdiplomstudium des Erhalts des Naturerbes an der Biotechnischen Fakultät in Ljubljana und am Birkbeck College der University of London entschlossen. Zur Zeit ist sie als freischaffende Journalistin und Dozentin tätig.

La creatività culturale e artistica fa parte della sua tradizione familiare (il nonno è compositore, la madre attrice e il padre scultore), così come il forte legame con la natura e con la montagna (entrambi i genitori erano alpinisti). Terminati gli studi di storia ed etnologia, ha lavorato per quasi vent'anni a TV Slovenija come autrice e redattrice di documentari. Per la serie "Gore in ljudje" (Montagne e gente), di cui è autrice, ha ricevuto il premio Viktor per gli eccellenti risultati mediatici, nonché vari altri premi all'estero, in occasione di festival del cinema. Spinta dal desiderio di approfondire in modo scientifico la sua passione per la natura e per il mondo selvaggio (montagne, mare, boschi e grotte), ha deciso di intraprendere uno studio post-laurea in tutela del patrimonio naturale presso la Facoltà di Biotecnica di Lubiana e alla Birkbeck College University di Londra.
Conclusa l'esperienza di TV Slovenija, lavora attualmente come giornalista free-lance e conferenziera.

Bogdan Kladnik

BOGDAN KLADNIK, born 1960 in Ljubljana, blames his love for nature and books on his parents, for his family often went hiking to the hills, and he used to help his father with proofing his books. As a student of medicine he became very well acquainted with human anatomy - which he makes the most of, in spite of his years and his injuries, in his mountaineering, kayaking, karate, polar expeditions, his explorations of gorges and waterfalls and his pot-holing. As photographer, editor, designer, writer and publisher all in one person, he has for 15 years been involved in producing and marketing Slovene books. He is the author and publisher of 32 photo-monographs about the Slovene natural and cultural heritage.

BOGDAN KLADNIK - geb. 1960 in Ljubljana, führt seine Liebe zur Natur und zu den Büchern auf seine Eltern zurück. Bergwanderungen mit der Familie und die Mitarbeit an den Büchern seines Vaters, eines bekannten Physikers, erwiesen sich als prägend. Das Medizinstudium machte ihn mit der menschlichen Anatomie vertraut, was ihm noch heute in seiner Tätigkeit als Bergsteiger zugute kommt oder wenn er in Polarexpeditionen, Karate, Schluchten, Höhlen und bei Wasserfällen unterwegs ist. Mehr als 15 Jahre arbeitet er nun schon als Fotograf, Lektor, Layouter, Autor und Verleger von Büchern in einer Person und kennt folglich die Nöte derjenigen, die mit Büchern handeln. Bogdan Kladnik ist Autor und Verleger von 32 Fotomonographien über Natur und Kultur in Slowenien.

BOGDAN KLADNIK, nato nel 1960 a Ljubljana, considera colpevoli del suo amore per la natura e per i libri i suoi genitori. La sua famiglia, infatti, dedicava molto tempo alle escursioni sui monti, mentre il padre, famoso fisico, si faceva aiutare da lui nella correzione dei suoi libri. Da studente di medicina non laureato, ha approfondito la sua conoscenza dell'anatomia umana che, nonostante gli anni e le varie esperienze, sfrutta ancora oggi con successo nel canottaggio, nel karaté, nell'alpinismo, nelle spedizioni polari, nell'esplorazione di gole e cascate e nella speleologia.
In qualità di fotografo, redattore, designer, scrittore ed editore, tutto in un'unica persona, si occupa già da 15 anni della produzione e della vendita di libri sloveni. È autore ed editore di 32 monografie fotografiche sul patrimonio naturale e culturale della Slovenia.